THE PILGRIMS DIDN'T CELEBRATE THE FIRST THANKSGIVING

EXPOSING MYTHS ABOUT COLONIAL HISTORY

BY JULIA McDONNELL

Gareth Stevens
PUBLISHING

Please visit our website, www.garethstevens.com. For a free color catalog of all our high-quality books, call toll free 1-800-542-2595 or fax 1-877-542-2596.

Library of Congress Cataloging-in-Publication Data

Names: McDonnell, Julia, 1979- author.
Title: The pilgrims didn't celebrate the first Thanksgiving : exposing myths
  about colonial history / Julia McDonnell.
Description: New York : Gareth Stevens Publishing, 2017. | Series: Exposed!
  Myths about early American history | Includes index.
Identifiers: LCCN 2016037999| ISBN 9781482457339 (library bound book) | ISBN
  9781482457315 (pbk. book) | ISBN 9781482457322 (6 pack)
Subjects: LCSH: United States–History–Colonial period, ca.
  1600-1775–Juvenile literature. | United States–History–Errors,
  inventions, etc.–Juvenile literature.
Classification: LCC E187.2 .M33 2017 | DDC 973.2–dc23
LC record available at https://lccn.loc.gov/2016037999

First Edition

Published in 2017 by
Gareth Stevens Publishing
111 East 14th Street, Suite 349
New York, NY 10003

Designer: Sarah Liddell
Editor: Therese Shea

Photo credits: Cover, p. 1 GraphicaArtis/Contributor/Archive Photos/Getty Images; background texture used throughout IS MODE/Shutterstock.com; ripped newspaper used throughout STILLFX/Shutterstock.com; photo corners used throughout Carolyn Franks/Shutterstock.com; p. 5 Kean Collection/Staff/Archive Photos/Getty Images; p. 7 George Burba/Shutterstock.com; p. 9 Jon Bilous/Shutterstock.com; p. 11 (main) Ken Welsh/Getty Images; p. 11 (wood engraving) MarmadukePercy/Wikimedia Commons; p. 13 Charles Phelps Cushing/ClassicStock/Getty Images; p. 15 (Provincetown) LagunaticPhoto/Shutterstock.com; p. 15 (Plymouth Rock) Suchan/Shutterstock.com; p. 17 DEA/A. DAGLI ORTI/Contributor/De Agostini/Getty Images; p. 19 Stefano Bianchetti/Contributor/Corbis Historical/Getty Images; p. 21 (house remains) Boston Globe/Contributor/Boston Globe/Getty Images; p. 21 (house) Ogram/Wikimedia Commons; p. 23 Felix Lipov/Shutterstock.com; p. 25 © iStockphoto.com/duncan1890; p. 27 (map) Stock Montage/Contributor/Archive Photos/Getty Images; p. 27 (main) PhotoQuest/Contributor/Archive Photos/Getty Images; p. 29 Clindberg/Wikimedia Commons.

Printed in China

CPSIA compliance information: Batch #CW17GS: For further information contact Gareth Stevens, New York, New York at 1-800-542-2595.

CONTENTS

Words in the glossary appear in **bold** type the first time they are used in the text.

TRUE, FALSE, OR SOMETHING IN BETWEEN?

Who discovered America? What was life like for the first colonists? How and where was the first Thanksgiving **celebrated**? You may think you know . . . but you may be wrong!

Historical facts can be misunderstood, changed, or forgotten as they're shared through the years. Sometimes that happens by accident, and sometimes people do it on purpose in order to get others to think a certain way. As time passes, people may begin to believe **myths** rather than facts. That's often true of American colonial history.

In 1492, Columbus only sailed to islands: the Bahamas, Cuba, and Hispaniola. It wasn't until his third trip, in 1498, that he reached a **continent**, arriving at what's now Venezuela in South America.

You might think you know that Columbus sailed the Niña, Pinta, and Santa Maria to the Americas. That's partly true. Santa Maria was nicknamed La Gallega. Niña's real name was actually Santa Clara, and Pinta's real name is unknown!

COLUMBUS'S CLAIM TO FAME

THE MYTH: CHRISTOPHER COLUMBUS DISCOVERED AMERICA.

THE FACTS:

Christopher Columbus didn't discover the land that would become America. Millions of native people were already living there. Vikings from Greenland were the first Europeans known to have set foot on the North American continent. They landed around the year 1000.

Columbus gets the praise for the discovery because his travels opened up this territory to European countries. This led to European settlement in the "New World" and the beginning of the colonial period.

Newfoundland's L'Anse aux Meadows National Historic Site offers a model of the Viking settlement. Vikings were ancient people from northern Europe known for trading, raiding, and exploring.

WHY "AMERICA"?

Columbus believed he had reached the East Indies, but Italian explorer Amerigo Vespucci recognized Columbus had reached a continent unknown to Europeans. In Vespucci's honor, mapmakers in the 1500s named the territory "America."

7

THE RACE TO AMERICA

THE MYTH: FOUNDED IN 1620, PLYMOUTH, MASSACHUSETTS, WAS THE FIRST EUROPEAN COLONY IN THE NEW WORLD.

THE FACTS:

The people of St. Augustine, Florida—a city still standing today—would disagree. Their city was established in 1565 by Spain. The Dutch had lived in the New Netherland colony (now New York) since 1614. Because much of the New World was won by England later, other countries' colonial histories are often forgotten.

Even before Plymouth, the British founded Jamestown in Virginia in 1607. Other British colonies were settled, but later deserted, such as the Roanoke Colony in North Carolina.

This is the fort Castillo de San Marcos in St. Augustine. Think of how different the United States might be today if Spanish colonies had been more successful.

DON'T FORGET FRANCE

Well before Plymouth, the French had short-lived colonies in Florida and Texas. They had better luck creating New France, a land that reached from Canada south to the Gulf of Mexico.

MADE-UP LOVE MATCH

THE MYTH: POCAHONTAS AND JOHN SMITH FELL IN LOVE, AND SHE SAVED HIS LIFE.

THE FACTS:

The member of the Powhatan tribes known as "Pocahontas" was only about 11 years old when the British arrived in Virginia in 1607. John Smith was a leader of Jamestown's colonists and twice her age. According to him, the Powhatan people held him prisoner and sentenced him to death. Just before he could be killed, she saved him.

Some think it's possible that whatever happened was simply a welcoming **ceremony.** The Powhatan girl and Smith certainly didn't fall in love!

Pocahontas took the name "Rebecca" before marrying Englishman John Rolfe in 1614. This wood **engraving** (right) was made of her in England in 1616.

POCAHONTAS

JOHN ROLFE

MATOAKA ALS REBECCA FILIA POTENTISS : PRINC : POWHATANI IMP : VIRGINIA.

A WOMAN OF MANY NAMES

"Pocahontas" was the Powhatan girl's nickname! She was better known as "Matoaka" among her people. There are disagreements about the nickname's meaning. It could have meant "spoiled child" or "playful one." European historians used her nickname in their records, though.

THE MYTHIC MAYFLOWER

THE MYTH: THE *MAYFLOWER* WAS A LARGE SHIP OF PILGRIMS READY TO START OVER IN THE NEW WORLD.

THE FACTS:

The *Mayflower* was only about 100 feet (30.5 m) long and 25 feet (7.6 m) wide. However, it held 102 **passengers** and about 30 crewmembers! Fewer than half of the passengers were Pilgrims. These were people called Separatists who had split from the Church of England. They wanted a new place to practice their religion. The other passengers were seeking adventure or wealth in the New World.

Life on the ship was cold, wet, and overcrowded. Illnesses spread, and lack of good food weakened the passengers.

MAYFLOWER TRAGEDY

Once the 66-day journey was complete, the passengers still lived on board the *Mayflower* through the winter. Only half survived that winter.

Mayflower II, a copy of the original, can be seen—and boarded!—in Plymouth, Massachusetts.

A LEGENDARY ROCK

THE MYTH: THE PILGRIMS LANDED AT PLYMOUTH ROCK.

THE FACTS:

When the Pilgrims reached the New World in 1620, they stepped onto North American soil for the first time. But no accounts include Plymouth Rock or any rock at all.

It wasn't until over 120 years later that the grandson of a Pilgrim reported he'd been told the rock in Plymouth Harbor was an important piece of history. Despite the lack of proof for this, the story took hold. Pieces of rock were chipped away as people visited it over the years. Some are surprised at how small the rock is now!

The Plymouth Rock has been broken and put back together. The "1620" was cut into it in 1880.

PROVINCETOWN

MOTHER NATURE CHANGED HISTORY

Pilgrims first touched American soil in today's Provincetown on Cape Cod. They had planned to land further north, but bad weather forced them to Massachusetts—and with winter approaching, they decided to stay.

15

THE FIRST THANKSGIVINGS

THE MYTH: THE PILGRIMS AND NATIVE AMERICANS CELEBRATED AMERICA'S FIRST THANKSGIVING.

THE FACTS:

Native Americans had been holding ceremonies of thanks long before Europeans arrived. And European explorers before the Pilgrims had celebrations, too. The Spanish organized thanksgiving events in Texas in 1541 and 1598.

In 1607, Abnaki natives and British settlers in Maine shared a harvest feast. Florida claims colonists celebrated with the Timucuan tribe twice. It wasn't until the 1890s that the idea of the Pilgrims and Native Americans feasting together in 1621 became important to the Thanksgiving story.

PASS THE ALLIGATOR?

When Thanksgiving was celebrated in Florida, the menu could have featured tortoise, bear, and alligator!

17

THE MYTH: AT THE 1621 THANKSGIVING FEAST, PILGRIMS AND NATIVE AMERICANS SAT DOWN TOGETHER AT A LONG TABLE AND ATE A MEAL.

THE FACTS:

It probably wasn't fancy. Historians think the celebration was more like a big party. Guests came and went over several days. The Wampanoag had held their own harvest events. Celebrating with food, games, and music was familiar to them.

It's possible that the Pilgrims didn't even mean to include their native neighbors. Some think the Wampanoag heard guns fired in a celebration or in a hunt. Wampanoag chief Massasoit and 90 of his men arrived to see whether the settlers were preparing to attack—and stayed to eat!

In this picture, Massasoit greets the settlers, who welcome him with music.

BLACK, BUCKLES, AND BOOTS?

The Pilgrims are usually shown wearing dark colors and hats and shoes with **buckles**. In real life, their clothing was usually more colorful, and people didn't begin wearing buckles until later.

19

WHICH WITCHES CAME FIRST?

THE MYTH: SALEM, MASSACHUSETTS, HELD THE FIRST WITCH TRIALS IN THE COLONIES.

THE FACTS:

In 1692, the people of Salem Village hung at least 19 people for witchcraft. However, the people of Hartford, Connecticut, had witches on their minds years before that.

When 8-year-old Elizabeth Kelly of Hartford died unexpectedly in 1662, her parents wanted answers. Soon, many neighbors blamed each other for causing harm with magic! They believed the Bible told them to kill witches. Four were hanged. By 1697, more than 40 people in Connecticut were found guilty of witchcraft, and at least 11 were killed.

If you want to see where the Salem witchcraft craze began, visit the town of Danvers, not Salem. Danvers was known as Salem Village in 1692.

REMAINS OF THE HOUSE WHERE THE SALEM WITCHCRAFT CRAZE BEGAN

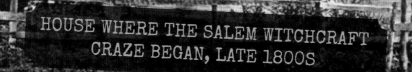

HOUSE WHERE THE SALEM WITCHCRAFT CRAZE BEGAN, LATE 1800S

SLAVES IN THE COLONIES

THE MYTH: ALL SLAVES IN AMERICA
WERE FROM AFRICA.

THE FACTS:

The first Africans were brought to America in 1619. Most slaves were kidnapped from Africa, but colonists enslaved people in other ways, too. Colonists captured Native Americans or bought them from tribes that had taken them as prisoners. There are even records of courts sentencing people to slavery.

Enslaving people from Africa became illegal in 1808. However, a child born to a mother who was a slave became one, too, so slavery continued in North America for decades.

NOT SLAVES, BUT NOT FREE

Most laborers that came to the colonies before 1680 were indentured servants. That means they agreed to work in exchange for the trip overseas, a place to sleep, and food. Some lived well—but others were treated poorly.

Most of North America's slaves were taken from a small area in the center of the west coast of Africa. Some were held in Ghana's Elmina Castle, shown here, a post used in the slave trade.

THE MYTH:
SLAVERY ONLY EXISTED IN THE SOUTH.

THE FACTS:

All 13 American British colonies allowed slavery. At one point, northern colonists owned 40,000 slaves, and slaves made up about 20 percent of New York City's population. Even **Founding Fathers** such as George Washington and Benjamin Franklin took part in the slave trade.

Northern slaves often lived in cities, working as laborers, **artisans,** and servants. Slave women often performed household jobs, while men did the physical work. In the South, both men and women slaves worked in the fields of large farms called plantations.

About 500,000 Africans forced into slavery came to the American colonies. About 10 million came to the Americas in all.

25

AMERICA'S FIRST FIGHTS

THE FACTS:

There were many **conflicts** among England, Spain, France, the Netherlands, and their colonies before American colonists fought the British for their freedom in the American Revolution. Sometimes the conflicts began over territory and events in the New World. However, some were part of larger European wars.

Many Native Americans chose sides and fought alongside the colonists. In fact, the British might not have won the French and Indian War (1754–1763) without Native American help.

MOST UNUSUAL NAME FOR A WAR

The War of Jenkins' Ear (1739–1748), fought between Spain and England, got its name when a Spanish soldier cut off British captain Robert Jenkins's ear. Jenkins was told to tell the British king that the same would be done to him.

A MAP of the
BRITISH DOMINIONS
IN
NORTH AMERICA,
according to the TREATY in 1763;
By Peter Bell, Geographer.
1772.

After the French and Indian War, France gave much of its territory east of the Mississippi River to England and the territory called Louisiana to Spain. France kept control of the city of New Orleans.

DIG DEEPER

Learning history isn't always as simple as reading a book or website. Sometimes, the writer of the history **influences** how the facts are recorded and remembered. If you asked Native Americans, slaves, women, and other people who didn't hold much power during the colonial period about events, their accounts might be very different.

Don't be afraid to study more and ask questions about what you've been taught. You never know what interesting things you might uncover!

The American Revolution ended in 1783, along with the colonial period of American history, with the signing of the Treaty of Paris.

AN AMERICAN COLONIAL TIMELINE

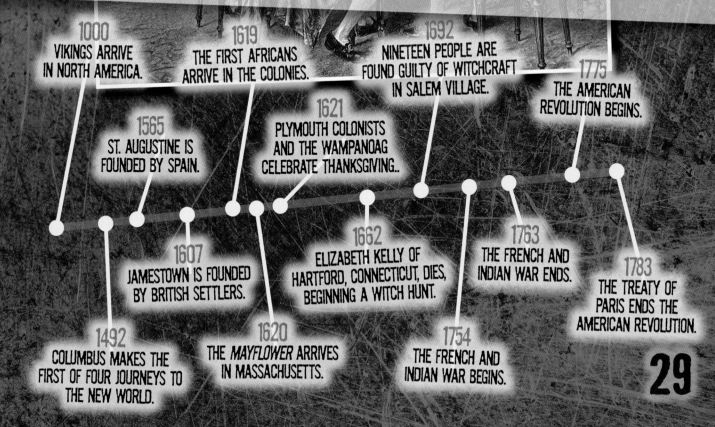

1000
VIKINGS ARRIVE IN NORTH AMERICA.

1619
THE FIRST AFRICANS ARRIVE IN THE COLONIES.

1692
NINETEEN PEOPLE ARE FOUND GUILTY OF WITCHCRAFT IN SALEM VILLAGE.

1775
THE AMERICAN REVOLUTION BEGINS.

1565
ST. AUGUSTINE IS FOUNDED BY SPAIN.

1621
PLYMOUTH COLONISTS AND THE WAMPANOAG CELEBRATE THANKSGIVING..

1607
JAMESTOWN IS FOUNDED BY BRITISH SETTLERS.

1662
ELIZABETH KELLY OF HARTFORD, CONNECTICUT, DIES, BEGINNING A WITCH HUNT.

1763
THE FRENCH AND INDIAN WAR ENDS.

1492
COLUMBUS MAKES THE FIRST OF FOUR JOURNEYS TO THE NEW WORLD.

1620
THE *MAYFLOWER* ARRIVES IN MASSACHUSETTS.

1754
THE FRENCH AND INDIAN WAR BEGINS.

1783
THE TREATY OF PARIS ENDS THE AMERICAN REVOLUTION.

GLOSSARY

artisan: a worker who practices a trade or skilled craft

buckle: a tool that keeps two ends of a belt together

celebrate: to do something special to honor or enjoy an event

ceremony: a formal act or acts that are part of an event

conflict: a fight, battle, or war

continent: one of the seven great landmasses on Earth

engraving: a picture made by the act of cutting into metal or wood, inking the surface of the metal or wood, and pressing paper against it

Founding Father: a man who had an important part in creating the government of the United States

influence: to affect or change something in an indirect but usually important way

myth: an idea or story that is believed by many people but that is not true

passenger: a person who is traveling in a car, bus, train, ship, or airplane and who is not working on it

FOR MORE INFORMATION

BOOKS

Cook, Peter. *You Wouldn't Want to Sail on the Mayflower! A Trip That Took Entirely Too Long.* New York, NY: Franklin Watts, 2014.

Hinman, Bonnie. *The Scoop on School and Work in Colonial America.* North Mankato, MN: Capstone Press, 2012.

Raum, Elizabeth. *The Dreadful, Smelly Colonies: The Disgusting Details About Life During Colonial America.* Mankato, MN: Capstone Press, 2010.

WEBSITES

Colonial and Early America
www.loc.gov/teachers/classroommaterials/themes/colonial-america/students.html
Learn about early America by exploring maps, papers, drawings, and more.

Plimoth Plantation
www.plimoth.org
Go back in time to visit the colony and see how the Pilgrims and Native Americans lived.

INDEX